CONGREGATION
FOR INSTITUTES OF CONSECRATED LIFE
AND SOCIETIES OF APOSTOLIC LIFE

Cor Orans

Instruction on the Implementation
of the Apostolic Constitution
Vultum Dei quaerere
on Women's Contemplative Life

Print on Demand Edition 2021

On the cover:

MARKO IVAN RUPNIK, *Washing of the Feet,* detail
Church of Our Lady on Mount Carmel, Snagov (Romania)

00120 Città del Vaticano
Tel. 0669845780
e-mail: commerciale.lev@spc.va
www.libreriaeditricevaticana.va
[illegible]

ISBN 978-88-266-0649-1

INTRODUCTION

PRAYING HEART, guardian of gratuity, wealth of apostolic fruitfulness and of a mysterious and multiform holiness is the feminine contemplative life in the Church. The contemplative life of nuns, rooted in the silence of the cloister, from its beginnings through a mysterious apostolic fruitfulness enriches the Church of Christ with fruits of grace and mercy[1].

With our gaze turned to this unique form of the *sequela Cristi*, Pope Pius XII, on November 21, 1950, published the Apostolic Constitution *Sponsa Christi Ecclesia*[2] with feminine monastic life as the object. In this document, the Roman Pontiff recognized the monasteries of nuns as true autonomous monasteries[3]

[1] Cf. FRANCISCUS PP., *Constitutio apsostolica Vultum Dei quaerere* (= *VDq*). *De vita contemplative monialium*, in *AAS* CVIII (2016), 838, n. 5; *Perfectae caritatis* (= *PC*) 7; can. 674 CJC.

[2] Cf. PIUS PP. XII, *Apostolic Constitution Sponsa Christi Ecclesia* (= *SCE*). *De sacro monialium instituto promovendo*, in *AAS* XXXXIII (1951), 5-23.

[3] Cf. *Statuta generalia monialium* (= *SGM*), art. VI, in *AAS* XXXXIII (1951), 17.

and advocated the birth of the Federations[4] as structures of communion to overcome the isolation of monasteries in order to favor the conservation of the common charism and collaboration in various forms of reciprocal help, giving indications for the *accommodata renovatio*[5] of what was defined as the Institute of nuns, above all on the issue of cloister[6]. In fact, Pope Pius XII anticipated for the monasteries of nuns what the Second Vatican Council would ask a few years later of all the religious institutes[7].

As Pope Pius XII himself recalled at the beginning of the Apostolic Constitution which, almost as a historical introduction, delineates the essential features of the various phases of female consecrated life in the Church[8] over the centuries, the intention and design of the founders, sanctioned by the competent authority of the Church, has enriched the Church, the Bride of Christ, with a multitude of charisms, modeling various forms of contemplative life in diverse

[4] Cf. *SCE*, 12; *SGM*, art. VII, in *AAS* XXXXIII (1951), 18-19.

[5] Cf. *SCE*, 10-11.

[6] Cf. *SCE*, 12; *SGM*, art. VII, in *AAS* XXXXIII (1951), 18-19.

[7] Cf. *Pc* 2.

[8] Cf. *SCE*, 6-11.

monastic traditions and different charismatic families[9].

The originality of the document, which dealt with the discipline/norms common to the Institute of nuns, of the autonomous monastery, and the Federation among autonomous monasteries, gave long life to the Apostolic Constitution *Sponsa Christi Ecclesia,* which remained in force even after the celebration of Vatican Council II and the promulgation of the Code of Canon Law, up to the present.

In fact, Pope Francis, by promulgating the Apostolic Constitution *Vultum Dei quaerere,* on June 29, 2016, to help the contemplatives reach the aim of their specific vocation, invited reflection and discernment on the precise content[10] tied to consecrated life in general and to the monastic tradition in particular, but he did not intend to abrogate *Sponsa Christi Ecclesia* that was derogated only in some points[11]. As a consequence, the two pontifical documents are to be held as normative in force for monasteries of nuns and must be read in a unitary vision.

Pope Francis, in the wake of the teaching of Pope Pius XII and reaffirmed by Ecumen-

[9] Cf. *SCE,* 8-9.

[10] Cf. *VDq,* 13-35.

[11] Cf. *VDq,* 13-35.

ical Vatican Council II, intended to present in *Vultum Dei quaerere* the intense and fruitful path taken by the Church in the last decades, in the light of the teachings of the same Council and considering the changed socio-cultural conditions[12].

As a consequence, from the moment that Institutes entirely dedicated to contemplation always occupy an eminent place in the mystical body of Christ "*no matter how urgent the need of the active apostolate, the members of these Institutes cannot be called to lend the help of their work in diverse pastoral ministries*" [13].

By the mandate of the Holy Father[14], the Congregation for Institutes of Consecrated Life and Societies of Apostolic Life has redacted the present Instruction on the implementation of the Apostolic Constitution *Vultum Dei quaerere*, offered "*to the Church, with particular reference to monasteries of the Latin Rite*" [15], an Instruction that intends to clarify the dispositions of the law, developing and determining the procedures for implementing it[16].

[12] Cf. *VDq*, 8.

[13] Can. 674 CJC.

[14] *VDq*, art. 14, § 1.

[15] *VDq*, art. 14, § 1.

[16] *VDq*, art. 14, § 1.

GENERAL NORMS

1. According to the law, the term *nuns,* in addition to the religious of solemn vows, refers to those who profess simple vows in monasteries, both perpetual as temporary. The Church, among the women consecrated to God through the profession of the evangelical counsels, designates only to nuns the commitment of public prayer, raising to God in its name the Divine Office as a praying community to be celebrated in chorus.

2. The legitimate name *nuns* is not opposed to: 1) the simple profession emitted legitimately in monasteries; 2) the exercise of apostolic works joined to contemplative life whether by approved institution and confirmed by the Holy See for some Orders, or for legitimate prescription or concession by the Holy See in favor of some monasteries.

3. All monasteries in which only simple vows are professed can ask the Holy See for the restoration of the solemn vows.

4. The particular form of religious life that nuns must live faithfully according to the charism of their Institute, and to which they are destined by the Church, is canonical contemplative life. The term *canonical contemplative life* does not mean the internal and theological one to which all the faithful are invited in the power of baptism, but rather the external profession of religious discipline that, whether through the exercises of piety, prayer, and mortification, or through the occupations which the nuns must attend to, is so ordered to interior contemplation that their whole life and all actions can easily and must efficaciously be imbued by the desire for it.

5. *Holy See* in the present Instruction refers to the Congregation for Institutes of Consecrated Life and Societies ofî Apostolic Life.

6. *Monastery sui juris* refers to the religious house of a female monastic community that, having the requisites for real autonomy of life, was legitimately erected by the Holy See and enjoys juridical autonomy under the law.

7. *Federation of monasteries* means a structure of communion among some autonomous monasteries of the same Institute, erected by the Holy See that approves the Statutes, so that in sharing the same charism, the federated monasteries overcome isolation and promote regular observance and contemplative life.

8. *Association of monasteries* is meant a structure of communion between several autonomous monasteries of the same Institute erected by the Holy See so that, in sharing the same charism, the associated monasteries collaborate among themselves according to the Statutes approved by the Holy See.

9. *Conference of monasteries* means a structure of communion among autonomous monasteries, belonging to diverse Institutes and present in the same region, erected by the Holy See that approves the Statutes, with the aim of promoting contemplative life and of favoring collaboration among the monasteries in particular geographical or linguistic contexts.

10. *Confederation* means a structure of connection among Federations of monasteries, erected by the Holy See that approves the Statutes, for the study of themes relative to contemplative life in relation to the same charism, to give unitary direction and a certain coordination to the activity of the individual Federations[17].

[17] *VDq*, art. 9, § 4.

11. *International Commission* means a centralized organ of service and of study for the benefit of nuns of the same Institute, erected or recognized by the Holy See that approves its Statutes, for the study of themes relative to contemplative life in relation to the same charism[18].

12. *Monastic Congregation* means a structure of government, erected by the Holy See, among several autonomous monasteries of the same Institute, under the authority of a President, who is the Major Superior according to law[19], and of a general chapter, that in the monastic Congregation is the supreme authority, in accordance with the Constitutions approved by the Holy See.

13. The provisions of this Instruction for the *Federation of Monasteries* are equally valid for the *Association of Monasteries* and for the *Conference of Monasteries,* taking into account their unique nature and their own Statutes approved by the Holy See.

14. The provisions of this Instruction for the Federation of Monasteries apply *congrua congruis referendo* to the women monastic

[18] *VDq*, art. 9, § 4.

[19] Cf. can. 620 CJC.

Congregations, unless otherwise provided by the universal and proper law, or does not otherwise arise from the context or nature of things.

I.

THE AUTONOMOUS MONASTERY

15. The monastery *sui juris* is a religious house which enjoys legal autonomy: its Superior is a Major Superior[20], its community is permanently established for the number and quality of the members; by law it is the place of the novitiate and of formation, is considered a public juridical person, and its assets are ecclesiastical goods.

16. The Church recognizes for every monastery *sui juris* a proper juridical autonomy of life and of government, through which the community of nuns can enjoy its own discipline and be able to preserve its character and protect its identity[21].

17. The autonomy of the monastery favors stability of life and the internal unity of each community, ensuring the best conditions for the life of the nuns, according to

[20] Cf. can. 613, § 2 and 620 CJC.

[21] Cf. can. 586, § 1 CJC.

the spirit and the nature of the Institute to which they belong[22].

18. In order to obtain juridical autonomy for a monastery of nuns, it must presuppose a real autonomy of life, that is, the ability to manage the life of the monastery in all its dimensions (vocational, formative, governmental, relational, liturgical, economic...). In this case, an autonomous monastery is alive and vital[23].

19. A monastery of nuns, as every religious house, is erected while keeping in mind its usefulness for the Church and for the Institute[24].

I. Foundation

20. The foundation of a monastery of nuns, keeping in mind what is established in no. 39 of the present Instruction, can take place either by a single monastery or through the action of the Federation, as established by the Federal Assembly.

21. The foundation on the part of a single monastery must be an expression of the

[22] Cf. *VDq*, 28.

[23] Cf. *Ibidem*.

[24] Cf. can. 610 CJC.

maturity of the community of a living and vital autonomous monastery, which generates a new community capable of being, in turn, a witness of the primacy of God, according to the spirit and the nature of the Institute to which the community belongs.

22. The foundation established by the Federation must be an expression of the communion among the monasteries and express the will to spread the contemplative life, especially in particular churches where this is not present.

23. In discerning the foundation of a new monastery on the part of a single monastery, the Federal President and the religious Assistant intervene to help the Superior of the founding monastery. The discernment on the foundation of a new monastery by the Federation is made within the framework of the Federal Assembly.

24. The opportunity for the foundation of a monastery of nuns must be prudently considered, especially if the foundation is carried out by a single monastery, so that the founding community is not weakened, carefully considering the choice of the place, because this choice involves a different and particular form of preparation for the foundation and the members of the future community.

25. In choosing the country in which the foundation is to take place, consideration must be given if monastic life is already present, all necessary and useful information must be acquired, above all on the presence and vitality of the Catholic Church, on vocations to consecrated life, on the religious attitude of the population, and on the possibility of future vocations for the new foundation.

26. In choosing the place for the foundation, the necessary conditions must be ensured to guarantee the nuns the possibility of an adequate sustenance, of regularly conducting contemplative life in the monastery[25], and of favoring relations among the monasteries.

27. In choosing the place of the foundation, particular attention must be paid to the needs of the sacramental and spiritual life of the new monastery, because the lack of clergy in some particular churches does not always allow the appointment of a priest who has the competence and spiritual sensitivity to accompany the community of a monastery of nuns.

[25] Cf. can. 610 CJC.

28. In choosing the place of the foundation, the aspect of separation from the world must be especially foreseen and cared for given the public witness that the nuns are obliged to render to Christ and the Church in contemplative life, according to the nature and aims of the Institute of belonging[26], in the discipline of cloister, provided by law[27].

29. The monastery of nuns is founded with a capitular decision of the community of an autonomous monastery or with a decision of the Federal Assembly, and the sending of at least five nuns, at least three of them of solemn vows, with the prior written consent of the diocesan Bishop[28] and the authorization of the Holy See.

30. The foundation does not, however, enjoy any autonomy; until the time of the canonical erection as monastery *sui juris*, it is entirely dependent on the founding monastery or on the Federation.

31. The local Superior of the foundation is a nun of solemn vows, suitable for the exercise of the service of authority, appointed

[26] Cf. can. 607, § 3 CJC.

[27] Cf. can. 667, §§ 2-3 CJC; cf. *VDq*, 31.

[28] Cf. can. 609, § 1 CJC.

by the Major Superior of the founding monastery or by the Federal President, in accordance with their proper law.

32. The nuns of the foundation, who must freely adhere in writing to this project, retain capitular rights in their own monastery which remain suspended in their exercise until the erection of the new monastery.

33. The Major Superior of the founding monastery or the Federal President may ask the Holy See that the foundation be established as the place of the novitiate in the presence of a community of at least five professed nuns with solemn vows, assuring the presence of a nun of solemn vows legitimately appointed by the Major Superior of the founding monastery or the Federal President, who performs the task of novice mistress.

34. If the foundation was made by a single monastery, until the time of the erection as an autonomous monastery, candidates are admitted to the novitiate, novices to temporary profession, and temporary professed to solemn profession by the Major Superior of the founding monastery, in accordance with the universal and proper law.

35. If the foundation was made by the Federation, until the time of its erection as an autonomous monastery, candidates are admitted to the novitiate, novices to temporary profession, and temporary professed to solemn profession by the Federal President, with the consent of the Federal Council, after consulting the local Superior and the foundation community, in accordance with the universal law and the Statutes of the Federation.

36. The community of the foundation does not have a conventual chapter, but a local chapter and, until the time of erection as an autonomous monastery, profession will be emitted for the founding monastery – or for another monastery of reference established by the Federal President at the time of the foundation on the part of the Federation – although in view of the future erection of a new autonomous monastery.

37. The foundation, if erected in the place of the novitiate, becomes the place of formation for the temporary professed as well; therefore, it must ensure the presence of a nun of solemn vows, legitimately appointed by the Major Superior of the founding monastery or by the Federal President, who carries out the task of formation.

38. It is established that the appropriate time between the foundation and erection of a monastery of nuns will be fifteen years at most. After this period of time the Holy See, having heard the Superior of the founding monastery, the Federal President, the religious Assistant, and the competent Ordinary, must assess whether there is a well-founded hope of continuing the foundation to reach the canonical erection of the monastery or decree its end, according to the law.

II. Canonical Erection

39. A monastery of nuns is erected as a monastery *sui juris* at the request of the community of the founding monastery or by the decision of the Federal Council with the approval of the Holy See[29] in the presence of the following requirements:

a) a community that has given good testimony of fraternal life in common with "*the necessary vitality in living and transmitting the charism*"[30], composed of at least eight nuns of solemn vows, "*as long as most are not of advanced age*"[31];

b) besides the number, special skills are required of some nuns of the community who must be able to assume: as Superior, the

[29] Cf. can. 609, § 2 CIC.

[30] *VDq*, art. 8, § 1.

[31] *Ibidem.*

service of authority; as formator, the initial formation of candidates; as financial administrator, the administration of the goods of the monastery;

c) rooms adapted to the lifestyle of the community, to ensure that the nuns can regularly lead the contemplative life according to the nature and spirit of their Institute;

d) economic conditions that guarantee the community itself can provide for the needs of daily life.

These criteria must be considered in their entirety and from an overall perspective[32].

40. It is the responsibility of the Holy See to evaluate the presence of these requisites, after carefully considering the request transmitted by the Major Superior of the founding monastery or by the Federal President, and having acquired, on its part, other information.

41. The erection of a monastery of nuns cannot proceed if prudence does not indicate it can adequately provide for the needs of the community[33] and there is no certainty in regard to the stability of the monastery.

[32] *VDq*, art. 8, § 1.

[33] Cf. can. 610, § 2 CJC.

42. Bearing in mind the particular apostolate of the contemplative communities with the witness of their consecrated life, which the nuns are called to render to Christ and to the Church, and the eminent place that they occupy in the mystical Body of Christ, the nuns cannot be called on to lend the help of their work in the various pastoral ministries nor should they accept them.

43. Autonomy of life, a constant prerequisite for maintaining juridical autonomy, must be constantly verified by the Federal President[34] who, when in her judgment a monastery lacks autonomy of life, must inform the Holy See in view of the nomination of an *ad hoc* commission[35].

44. The autonomous monastery is governed by a Major Superior, designated according to the norm of the proper law.

45. When the number of professed members of solemn vows falls to five, the community of said monastery loses the right to the election of its Superior. In this case, the Federal President is obliged to inform the Holy See in view of appointing the *ad hoc* commis-

[34] Cf. *VDq*, art. 8, § 1.
[35] Cf. *VDq*, art. 8, § 2.

sion[36] and whoever has the right to preside over the elective chapter, subject to authorization from the Holy See, will proceed to the appointment of an Administrator Superior, after having heard the members of the community individually.

46. The autonomous monastery has the capacity to acquire, possess, administer, and dispose of temporal goods, in accordance with the universal and proper law[37].

47. The assets of the autonomous monastery are administered by a nun of solemn vows, with the office of Financial Administrator, constituted according to the proper law and distinct from the Major Superior of the monastery[38].

48. The community of the monastery considers the goods in its possession as gifts received from God through benefactors and the work of the community, as a necessary and useful means to achieve the proper ends of the Institute to which they belong, always respecting the requirements of the profession of the evangelical counsel of poverty by public vow.

[36] Cf. *VDq*, art. 8, § 2.
[37] Cf. can. 634, § 1 CJC.
[38] Cf. can. 636 CJC.

49. Extraordinary administrative acts are those that exceed the usual needs for the maintenance and work of the community and for the normal maintenance of the buildings of the monastery.

50. Within the ordinary administration, the Major Superior and the Financial Administrator of the monastery carry out valid administrative acts within the confines of their roles.

51. For expenses and acts of extraordinary administration, the authorization of the Council of the monastery and of the conventual Chapter is necessary according to the value of the sum, to be determined by the proper law.

52. In derogation from can. 638, § 4 CJC, for the validity of the alienation and of any other transaction by which the patrimonial situation of the monastery could be damaged, the written permission of the Major Superior is required with the consent of the Council or of the conventual Chapter, depending on the value of the sale and the transaction, and the opinion of the Federal President[39].

[39] Exemption approved in specific form by the Holy Father.

53. If it deals with a transaction or sale whose value exceeds the sum set by the Holy See for the individual regions or of votive donations made to the Church or of precious items of historical and artistic value, the permission of the Holy See is also required.

III. Affiliation

54. Affiliation is a particular form of help that the Holy See establishes in particular situations in favor of the community of a monastery *sui juris* which has only an asserted autonomy, but in reality, very precarious or, in fact, non-existent.

55. Affiliation is configured as a juridical support that must assess whether the inability to manage the life of the autonomous monastery in all its dimensions is only temporary or is irreversible, helping the community of the affiliated monastery to overcome difficulties or to put in place what is necessary to bring about the suppression of this monastery.

56. In these cases, it is up to the Holy See to evaluate the opportunity of setting up an *ad hoc* commission formed by the Ordinary, the Federation President, the Federal

Assistant, and the Major Superior of the monastery[40].

57. Through affiliation, the Holy See suspends the *status* of autonomous monastery, rendering it *donec aliter provideatur* a house dependent on another autonomous monastery of the same Institute or of the Federation, according to what is established in the present Instruction and any other provisions on the matter given by the Holy See itself.

58. The Major Superior of the autonomous affiliating monastery or the Federal President is constituted Major Superior of the affiliated monastery.

59. The local Superior of the affiliated monastery is a nun of solemn vows, named *ad nutum* by the Major Superior of the autonomous monastery or by the Federal President[41], with the consent of the respective Council, having heard the nuns of the community of the affiliated monastery. Said local Superior is constituted legal representative of the affiliated monastery.

60. The affiliated monastery can accept candidates, but the novitiate and initial for-

[40] *VDq*, art. 8, § 2.

[41] Cf. *VDq*, art. 8, § 3.

mation must be performed in the affiliating monastery or in another monastery established by the Federation.

61. The candidates of the affiliated monastery are admitted to the novitiate, the novices to temporary profession, and the temporary professed to solemn profession by the Major Superior of the affiliating monastery, having heard the community of the affiliated monastery and obtained the favorable vote of the conventual Chapter of the affiliating monastery or of the Federal President with the consent of her Council.

62. Profession will be emitted for the affiliated monastery.

63. During the time of affiliation, the finances of the two monasteries are administered distinctly.

64. The celebration of the conventual Chapter is suspended in the affiliated monastery, but the possibility of calling local Chapters remains unaffected.

IV. Transfer

65. By transfer we mean the translocation of a monastic community from its own location to another for a just cause, without modifying the juridical *status* of the monastery, the composition of the community, and the holders of the various offices.

66. To perform the transference, it is necessary to:

a) obtain a decision of the monastery conventual Chapter by a two-thirds majority of the votes;

b) advise in a convenient time the Bishop in whose diocese the monastery that will be left is located;

c) obtain the prior written consent of the Bishop of the diocese where the community of nuns is transferring;

d) submit the request for transfer to the Holy See, engaging in the conveyance of assets owned by the monastery community, in accord with the canonical and civil norms on the matter.

V. Suppression

67. Affiliation can be an opportunity for recovery and rebirth when autonomy of life is partially compromised. If the situation of incapacity is irreversible, the solution, as painful as it is necessary, is the suppression of the monastery.

68. A monastery of nuns that cannot express, according to the contemplative nature and finality of the Institute, the particular public witness to Christ and to the Church His Bride, must be suppressed, keeping in mind the usefulness to the Church and to the Institute to which the monastery belongs.

69. In these cases, it is up to the Holy See to evaluate the opportunity of setting up an *ad hoc* commission formed by the Ordinary, by the Federation President, the Federal Assistant, and by the Major Superior of the monastery[42].

70. Among the criteria that can contribute to determine a judgment concerning the suppression of a monastery, after having examined all the circumstances, the following points should be considered as a whole: the number of nuns, the advanced age of the majority of the members, the real capacity for government and formation, lack of candidates for a number of years, lack of the necessary vitality in living and transmitting the charism in dynamic fidelity[43].

[42] *VDq*, art. 8, § 2.

[43] Cf. *VDq*, art. 8, § 1; John Paul II, *Consecrated Life. Post-Synodal Apostolic Exhortation on the Consecrated Life* (= *VC*), Roma, 25 March 1996, 36-37.

71. A monastery of nuns is only suppressed by the Holy See after having acquired the opinion of the diocesan Bishop[44] and, if it seems opportune, having heard the opinion of the Federal President, of the religious Assistant, and of the religious Ordinary, if the monastery is associated according to the norm of can. 614 CJC.

72. The assets of the suppressed monastery, respecting the will of the founders and donors, follow the surviving nuns and go, in proportion, to the monasteries that receive them, unless otherwise provided by the Holy See[45] which may dispose, in individual cases, of a portion of the assets to be given to charity, to the particular church within whose boundaries the monastery is located, to the Federation, and to the "*Fund for the nuns*".

73. In the event of the suppression of a totally extinct monastery, when there are no surviving nuns, unless otherwise provided by the Holy See[46], the destination of the suppressed monastery's assets, in compliance with canon and civil law, go to the re-

[44] Cf. can. 616, § 1 and § 4 CJC.

[45] Cf. can. 616, § 2 CJC.

[46] Cf. can. 616, § 2 CJC.

spective higher juridical person, that is, to the Federation of monasteries or to another structure of communion among the monasteries equal to it or to the female monastic Congregation.

VI. Ecclesial Vigilance of the Monastery

74. Each structure of communion or government in which female monasteries can be configured, are guaranteed the necessary and due supervision, exercised principally – but not exclusively – through the regular visit of an authority external to the monasteries themselves.

75. Under the universal and proper law, the service of supervision corresponds to:

a) the President of the female monastic Congregation in reference to the communities of the congregated monasteries;

b) the Major Superior of the male associated institute, who is called the religious Ordinary, in reference to the community of the juridically associated female monastery, according to the law[47];

c) the diocesan Bishop in reference to the communities of monasteries entrust-

[47] Cf. can. 614 CJC.

ed to his special vigilance according to the norm of law[48] present in his own particular church.

76. Each female monastery is entrusted to the vigilance of a single authority, since the regime of simultaneous and cumulative "*double dependence*", that is, of the Bishop and of the regular Superior, present in various canons of the Code of Canon Law of 1917, is no longer present in the Code of Canon Law.

77. As regards the monasteries of nuns united in the monastic Congregation, the scope and concrete methods for carrying out the service of vigilance are to be drawn from the Constitutions of the female monastic Congregation, approved by the Holy See.

78. As regards the monasteries of juridically associated nuns, the scope and modalities for carrying out the service of vigilance by the religious Ordinary are established in their own Constitutions, approved by the Holy See, in which must be defined the rights and duties of the associate Superior and of the associated female monas-

[48] Cf. can. 615 CJC.

tery, according to their own spirituality and traditions.

79. As far as possible, the legal association of monasteries of nuns to the corresponding male order should be encouraged[49] in order to protect the identity of the charismatic family.

80. Congregated monasteries and juridically associated monasteries, however, remain bound to the diocesan Bishop as established by the universal law and reported in no. 83 of the present Instruction.

81. As regards the female monasteries entrusted to the particular vigilance of the diocesan Bishop, this is expressed in respect to the monastery community mainly in the cases established by the universal law; as the diocesan Bishop, he:

a) presides over the conventual Chapter that elects the Major Superior [50];

b) carries out the regular visit of the monastery, also with regard to internal discipline[51], taking into account the provisions of this Instruction;

[49] Cf. *VDq*, art. 9, § 4.

[50] Cf. can. 625, § 2 CJC.

[51] Cf. can. 628, § 2 n. 1 CJC.

c) examines, as the Local Ordinary, the annual report of the financial administration of the monastery[52];

d) in derogation from can. 638, § 4 CJC, gives as Local Ordinary, his written consent for particular administrative acts, if established by its proper law [53];

e) confirms the indult of definitive departure from the monastery, granted to a temporary professed member by the Major Superior with the consent of her Council[54];

f) issues the decree of dismissal of a nun, even of temporary vows[55].

82. These cases, expressed to delineate the scope and modality of the particular vigilance of the diocesan Bishop, form the basis of the scope and the vigilance of the religious Ordinary of the Associating Institute over the juridically associated female monastery and must be present in the Constitutions of the associated monastery.

[52] Cf. can. 637 CJC.

[53] Exemption approved by the Holy Father in a specific form

[54] Cf. can. 688, § 2 CJC.

[55] Cf. can. 699, § 2 CJC.

VII. Relations Between the Monastery and the Diocesan Bishop

83. All female monasteries, without prejudice to internal autonomy[56] and possible external exemption[57] are subject to the diocesan Bishop, who exercises pastoral care in the following cases:

a) the community of the female monastery is subject to the power of the Bishop[58], to whom it must devote respect and reverence in what concerns the public exercise of divine worship, the care of souls,[59] and the forms of apostolate corresponding to their character[60];

b) the diocesan Bishop[61], on the occasion of the pastoral visit or other paternal visits and even in case of necessity, can provide appropriate solutions himself[62] when he finds that there are abuses and after appeals made to the Major Superior have had no effect;

c) the diocesan Bishop intervenes in the erection of the monastery by giving written

[56] Cf. can. 586 CJC.
[57] Cf. can. 591 CJC.
[58] Cf. can. 678, § 1 CJC.
[59] Cf. can. 392; can. 680 CJC.
[60] Cf. can. 394; can. 673; can. 674; can. 612 CJC.
[61] Cf. can. 683, § 2 CJC.
[62] Cf. can. 1320 CJC.

consent before the approval of the Apostolic See is requested[63];

d) the diocesan Bishop intervenes, as local Ordinary, in the appointment of the chaplain[64] and, always as local Ordinary, in the approval of ordinary confessors[65]. Everything must take place "*considering the specificity of the proper charism and the needs of fraternal life in community*"[66];

e) the diocesan Bishop intervenes in the suppression of the monastery by expressing his opinion[67];

f) the exclaustrated nun refers to the diocesan Bishop, as the local Ordinary, and to her Superiors, remaining under their dependence and care[68];

g) the diocesan Bishop has the faculty, for a just cause, of entering the cloister and allowing other people to enter, with the consent of the Major Superior[69].

[63] Cf. can. 609 CJC.

[64] Cf. can. 567 CJC.

[65] Cf. can. 630, § 3 CJC.

[66] *VDq*, art. 6, § 2 CJC.

[67] Cf. can. 616, § 1 CJC.

[68] Cf. can. 687 CJC.

[69] Partial derogation from can. 667, § 4 CJC approved by the Holy Father in a specific form.

84. For congregated monasteries and associated monasteries, the points of pastoral care delineated above constitute the only possible forms of intervention by the diocesan Bishop, since the rights/duties of the President of the Congregation for the congregated monasteries and the rights/duties of the religious Ordinary of the Associating Institute towards the associated monastery must be safeguarded.

85. For monasteries entrusted to the particular vigilance of the diocesan Bishop, the points of pastoral care just outlined are to be added to those that the Code of Canon Law presents as expressions of particular vigilance, referred to in no. 81 of the present Instruction.

II.

THE FEDERATION OF MONASTERIES

I. Nature and End

86. The Federation is a structure of communion among monasteries of the same Institute erected by the Holy See so that monasteries which share the same charism do not remain isolated but keep it faithfully and, giving each other mutual fraternal help, live the indispensable value of communion[70].

87. The Federation is made up of several autonomous monasteries that have affinity of spirit and traditions and even if they are not necessarily configured according to a geographical criterion, as far as possible, they must not be geographically too distant[71].

88. The Holy See has the exclusive competence to erect, suspend, unite, and suppress the Federations[72] of monasteries of nuns.

[70] Cf. *VDq*, 28-30.

[71] Cf. *VDq*, art. 9, § 2.

[72] Cf. can. 582 CJC.

89. Likewise, the Holy See has the exclusive competence of ascribing an autonomous monastery to a Federation or allowing the passage of a monastery from one Federation to another of the same Institute.

90. The Federation of monasteries of nuns, by the source from which it derives and by the authority on which it directly depends and is governed, is of pontifical right, in accordance with canon law.

91. The Statutes of the Federation must conform not only to what is established by this Instruction, but also to the nature, laws, spirit, and traditions of the Institute to which they belong.

92. The Federation, in accordance with this Instruction and its Statutes, in the distinctiveness of its own charism, promotes contemplative life in the monasteries, guarantees assistance in initial and ongoing formation, as well as the exchange of nuns and material goods[73].

93. Pursuant to the provisions of the Apostolic Constitution *Vultum Dei quaerere,* all monasteries must initially enter a Federation[74].

[73] Cf. *VDq*, 30; art. 9, § 3.
[74] Cf. *VDq*, art. 9, § 1.

A monastery, for special reasons that are objective and motivated, with the vote of the conventual Chapter can ask the Holy See to be exempted from this obligation. The granting of such dispensation is reserved to the Holy See. A monastery, for objective and motivated reasons, with the vote of the conventual Chapter can ask the Holy See to no longer belong to a Federation. The Holy See must make an appropriate discernment before granting the exit from a Federation.

94. Once canonical erection has been obtained, the Federation seeks legal recognition also in the civil sphere and places its legal see in one of the monasteries belonging to it.

95. Several Federations of the same Institute, with the approval of the Holy See, can constitute a *Confederation* among them[75] to give a unitary direction and a certain coordination to the activity of the single Federations.

96. The Holy See can establish or approve an *International Commission* for each Institute with the aim of encouraging the study of themes related to the contemplative life in relation to its own charism[76].

[75] Cf. can. 582 CJC; *VDq*, art. 9, § 4.

[76] Cf. *VDq*, art. 9, § 4.

97. The legitimately established Federation is a public juridic person in the Church and is therefore able to acquire, possess, administer, and alienate temporal, movable and immovable goods, which are ecclesiastical assets, in accordance with the universal and proper law.

98. To keep alive and strengthen the union of monasteries, implementing one of the aims of the Federation, a certain communication of goods is encouraged among the monasteries, coordinated by the Federal President.

99. The communication of goods in a Federation is implemented through contributions, gifts, loans that monasteries offer other monasteries that have financial difficulties, and for the common needs of the Federation.

100. The Federation considers the assets in its possession as necessary and useful means to achieve its goals.

101. Each Federation establishes an economic fund to be able to carry out the Federation's aims. This fund serves to cover the ordinary expenses of the Federation itself and those relating to the formation of funds at the federal level, to support the necessities of the subsistence and health of the nuns, to maintain the buildings, and to support new foundations.

102. The economic fund is nourished by the free donations of the monasteries, by the donations of benefactors, and by revenues deriving from the alienation of the assets of suppressed monasteries, as established by the present Instruction[77].

103. The Federation's finances are managed by the Federal Council, presided over by the Federal President, who makes use of the collaboration of the Federal Financial Administrator.

104. As part of ordinary administration, the Federal President and the Financial Administrator of the Federation make purchases and carry out valid administrative tasks within the limits of their role.

105. For expenses and acts of extraordinary administration, the authorization of the Federal Council and of the Federal Assembly is required, according to the value of the sum established in the proper law. Each Federation in the Elective Assembly sets the sum for which it is necessary to have the authori-

[77] Cf. *VDq*, 30; art. 9, § 3.

zation of the Federal Council and the Federal Assembly.

106. If it is a negotiation or sale whose value exceeds the sum set by the Holy See for the individual regions or deals with votive donations made to the Church of precious items due to their historical and artistic value, the permission of the Holy See is also required.

107. The validity of the sale and any other negotiation, through which the financial situation of the Federation could suffer damage, requires the written permission of the Federal President with the consent of the Council or the Federal Assembly, depending on the value of the negotiation, established by the proper law.

108. In derogation from can. 638, § 4 CJC, for the validity of the alienation of the assets of the suppressed monasteries, the President of the Federation and the Federal Council, beyond the value of the asset to be alienated, always and exclusively requires written permission from the Holy See[78].

109. Unless otherwise provided by the Holy See[79], the Federation President disposes

[78] Exemption approved by the Holy Father in specific form.

[79] Cf. can. 616, § 2 CJC

of the proceeds from the alienation of the assets of the totally extinct monasteries belonging to the Federation, as established by this Instruction.

II. The Federal President

110. The President of the Federation, elected by the Federal Assembly in accordance with the Statutes of the Federation for a period of six years, is not a Major Superior and, in the exercise of her service, acts on the strength of what the present Instruction attributes to her[80] in accordance with the universal and proper law.

111. In exemption of can. 628, § 2, 1° CJC, the Federation President, within the established time, accompanies the Regular Visitator in the canonical visit to the federated monasteries as a Co-Visitator [81].

112. The President of the Federation, when it comes to the canonical visit to the community of her own monastery, will delegate a Federal Councilor as a Co-Visitator of the regular Visitator.

[80] Cf. *VDq*, art. 9, § 3.

[81] Exemption approved by the Holy Father in a specific form.

113. The President of the Federation, whenever the need requires it, can visit the communities of the federated monasteries accompanied by a Co-Visitator, chosen in turn from among the Councilors, and by the Financial Administrators of the Federation.

114. All other visits – maternal or sisterly – are agreed on with the Superior of the monastery.

115. The President of the Federation, at the end of the canonical visit, indicates in writing to the Major Superior of the monastery, the most suitable solutions for the cases and situations that emerged during the visit and informs the Holy See of everything.

116. During the canonical visit, the President of the Federation verifies how the items contained in the points listed in no. 12 and developed in nos. 13-35 of the Apostolic Constitution *Vultum Dei quaerere*, are lived[82] and if the inherent application rules, decided in the Federal Assemblies, are observed.

117. The Federation President, in particular, watches over initial and ongoing formation in the monasteries to see if it is in conformity with the charism proper to the

[82] Cf. *VDq*, art. 2, § 2.

Institute, so that every community may be a beacon that illumines the journey of the men and women of our time[83]. At the end of the visit, she will inform the Holy See about the real possibilities that the monastery has or does not have of guaranteeing initial formation.

118. The formation of the formators and their collaborators is entrusted in part to the monasteries and in part to the Federation, therefore, the President of the Federation is called to strengthen formation at the federal level[84] and to require the participation of those who exercise the service of formation; if this does not happen, she will refer the matter to the Holy See.

119. The President of the Federation provides the formation foreseen by the Federal Assembly for those who are called to exercise the service of authority[85] and requires their participation; if this does not happen, she will refer the matter to the Holy See.

120. The President of the Federation, having heard the opinion of the Federal Council, chooses the most appropriate plac-

[83] Cf. *VDq*, 36.

[84] Cf. *VDq*, art. 3, § 3.

[85] Cf. *VDq*, art. 7, § 1.

es to hold the specific formative courses for the formators and their collaborators, as well as those who are called to exercise the service of authority, establishing the duration of these courses in such a way that they are not detrimental to the needs of the contemplative life[86] and of the community.

121. When an autonomous monastery no longer possesses a real autonomy of life[87], it is the responsibility of the Federation President to report the matter to the Holy See.

122. When the Major Superior of a monastery denies a nun consent for the passage to another monastery of the same Institute, the Federation President, having made due discernment with her Council on the matter, communicates this to the Holy See, who decides what to do.

III. The Federal Council

123. The Federal Council is composed of four councilors elected by the Federal Assembly from among all the solemnly professed nuns of the monasteries of the Federation and remains in office for six years.

[86] Cf. *VDq*, art. 3, § 4.
[87] Cf. *VDq*, art. 8, § 1.

124. The Federal Council has jurisdiction over what is attributed to it by this Instruction[88] and what may be established in the Statutes; nevertheless, the Federation President can consult it whenever she sees fit.

125. The Federal Council is consulted by the Federation President at the end of each canonical visit, before sending in writing to the Major Superior of the monastery, the best solutions to the cases and situations that emerged during the visit.

126. The Federal Council expresses its opinion in choosing the most appropriate times and places to hold specific formation courses for the formators and their collaborators, as well as for those who are called to exercise the service of authority.

127. The Federal Council collaborates with the Federation President in drafting the *Report* on the state of the Federation and of the individual monasteries, to be sent to the Holy See at the end of the six-year term.

128. The Federal Council is consulted by the Federation President before sending the request for affiliation or suppression of a monastery to the Holy See.

[88] Cf. *VDq*, 9, § 3.

129. The Federal Council gives its consent to the choice of the Federal Formator who carries out and coordinates initial formation in common[89]. Likewise, for serious reasons, it expresses its consent for the removal of the Federal Formator.

130. In exemption of can. 686, § 2 CJC, the Federal Council gives its consent for the request of the indult of exclaustration for a nun of solemn vows, after the year granted by the Major Superior of the monastery, up to the completion of three years[90].

131. The Federal Council gives its consent for the request for the extension of the indult of exclaustration for a nun of solemn vows, to be requested from the Holy See[91]. Before presenting the matter to the Federal Council, the Federal President must obtain the written opinion of the Major Superior of the nun professed with solemn vows asking for the extension of the indult, expressed collegially together with the Council of the monastery, with the consent of the local Ordinary where the nun will have to live, and having acquired

[89] Cf. *VDq*, art. 3, § 7.

[90] Exemption approved by the Holy Father in a specific form.

[91] Exemption approved by the Holy Father in a specific form.

the opinion of the diocesan Bishop or of the competent religious Ordinary.

132. The Federal Council assumes the functions of the Council of the autonomous monastery when the latter, through affiliation, is entrusted to the Federation President in the process of accompaniment for the revitalization or for the suppression of the monastery[92].

IV. The Federal Assembly

133. The communion that exists among monasteries becomes visible in the Federal Assembly, a sign of unity in charity, whose primary task is to protect the charismatic patrimony of the Institute among the federated monasteries and to promote an adequate renewal in harmony with it, providing that no Federation of monasteries of nuns or Confederation of Federations represents the entire Institute.

134. The Federal President, the Federal Councilors, the Federal Financial Administrator, the Major Superior, and a Delegate from each autonomous federated monastery, elected by the conventual Chapter, are mem-

[92] Cf. *VDq*, art. 8, § 7.

bers of the Federal Assembly; the Federal Secretary functions solely as an actuary.

135. The Ordinary Federal Assembly is convened every six years and the federal offices are renewed in it.

136. The Intermediate Federal Assembly is convened every three years to verify the progress made and to adopt any remedies or changes within them.

137. If necessity requires or expediency suggests it, the Federal President, with the consent of the Federal Council, can convoke the Extraordinary Federal Assembly.

138. The Federal Assembly, both ordinary and interim, is convened by the President at least six months before the expiration of the six-year period or the completion of the three-year period.

139. The Extraordinary Federal Assembly is convened by the President two months before its celebration.

140. With the cessation of the office of the Federal President, by death or in other ways provided by law[93], the first Councilor convenes, within one month of the office's

[93] Cf. can. 184, § 1 CJC.

vacancy, the Extraordinary Federal Assembly, to be celebrated within two months of the convocation. In this case, the Federal Councilors and the Federal Financial Administrator are elected again.

141. The Federal Assembly:

a) receives the *Report* of the Federal President on the state of the Federation and of the individual monasteries;

b) elects the Federal President and the Federal Council;

c) elects the Federal Financial Administrator;

d) deals with issues of major importance;

e) makes decisions and issues norms that all nuns are required to observe, after the definitive approval of the Holy See;

f) develops for a six-year period, the common formation courses that each community is obliged to carry out;

g) promotes the creation of new foundations and the methods for implementing them, both as single monasteries and as a federation;

h) identifies a monastery as the place of initial common formation for the monasteries of the Federation[94];

[94] Cf. *VDq*, art. 3, § 7.

i) establishes a formation plan for those who are called to exercise the service of authority[95] and for the Formators[96].

V. The Federal Offices

142. The administration of the Federation is entrusted to the Federal Financial Administrator, elected by the Federal Assembly for six years.

143. The Federal Financial Administrator has the responsibility to carry out what is established by the Federal Council and collaborates with the Federation President, in the context of the regular Visit, in verifying the financial performance of the individual monasteries, noting their positive and critical aspects, data that must appear in the final *Report* of the visit.

144. The Federal Secretary is chosen by the Federation President and remains in office for six years; this office can be carried out by one of the Federal Councilors.

145. The Federal Secretary, as far as possible, resides in the monastery selected as the legal see of the Federation and retains the

[95] Cf. *VDq*, art. 7, § 1.

[96] Cf. *VDq*, art. 3, § 3.

documents there and keeps the Federation archives updated.

146. Following the indications of the Federation President, the Federal Secretary draws up the agenda and convenes the Federal Council, during which she acts as an actuary.

147. The Federal Secretary, following the indications of the Federation President, prepares the Federal Assembly.

148. The Federal Formator[97] is appointed *ad nutum* by the Federation President with the consent of the Federal Council. The Federal Formator may be removed from her office for serious reasons, by the Federation President with the consent of the same Council.

VI. The Religious Assistant

149. The Federation Assistant represents the Holy See for the Federation, but not for the individual monasteries that comprise it, and carries out his task faithfully following the provisions relating to this office and carrying out the task received within the limits of his competence.

[97] Cf. *VDq*, art. 3, § 7.

150. The Federation Assistant, since he participates to a certain extent in the jurisdiction of the Holy See, is a presbyter appointed by the Congregation for Institutes of Consecrated Life and Societies of Apostolic Life for one or more Federations.

151. The Federation Assistant is not a Major Superior and carries out his task in a spirit of collaboration and service towards the Federation by encouraging the preservation of the genuine spirit of the Institute and helping the President and her Council in the conduct of the Federation, especially in formation at the federal level and in solving the most important financial problems.

152. The appointment of the Federation Assistant is reserved to the Holy See, but the Federation has the faculty to present candidates.

153. The appointment of the Assistant is *ad nutum Sanctae Sedis.*

154. The Federation President, within the established time, is obliged to present to the Holy See the names of three possible candidates for the office of Federation Assistant, attaching the results of the previous consultations of the communities of the single monasteries of the Federation, the *curriculum* *vitae* of each candidate, her own opinion and that of the Federation Council, the *nulla osta* of the Ordinaries of the candidates. The Holy See reserves to itself, in the manner deemed most appropriate and convenient, to integrate information concerning candidates to the office of Assistant.

155. Each year, the Federation Assistant must send a brief report of his work, on the progress of the Federation, reporting any particular situations. At the conclusion of his mandate, the Assistant sends a more detailed report on the state of the Federation to the Congregation for Institutes of Consecrated Life and Societies of Apostolic Life.

III.

SEPARATION FROM THE WORLD

I. Concept and Relevance for Contemplative Life

156. Starting from the wordings of the Code[98], it is affirmed that the separation from the world characterizes the nature and purpose of the religious Institutes of consecrated life and corresponds to the Pauline dictate of not conforming to the mentality of this century[99], fleeing from every form of worldliness.

For the religious life, the cloister is a common obligation for all Institutes[100] and expresses the material aspect of separation from the world – which, however, does not exhaust its scope – contributing to create in every religious house an atmosphere and an environment favorable to recollection, neces-

[98] Cf. can. 607, § 3 CJC.

[99] Cf. *Rm* 12:2.

[100] Cf. can. 667, § 1 CJC.

sary for the life of each religious Institute, but particularly for those dedicated to contemplation.

157. In the contemplative life of nuns, the aspect of separation from the world deserves particular attention for the high esteem that the Christian community nurtures towards this kind of life, sign of the exclusive union of the Church-Bride with her Lord, supremely loved.

158. The life of contemplative nuns, engaged in prayer in a very special way, in order to keep the heart constantly turned towards the Lord, in asceticism, and in the fervid progress of spiritual life, is nothing other than a striving to the heavenly Jerusalem, an anticipation of the Eschatological Church, fixed on the possession and contemplation of the face of God.

159. The community of the monastery of nuns, placed as a city on the mountain top and a light on the lampstand[101], even in the simplicity of its life, visibly depicts the goal towards which the whole ecclesial community walks, ardent in action and dedicated to contemplation, it advances along the paths

[101] Cf. *Mt* 5:14-15.

of time with eyes fixed on the future recapitulation of everything in Christ.

160. The material aspect of separation from the world has a particular manifestation in the cloister, which is the place of the Church's intimacy because, in the light of the particular vocation and ecclesial mission, the cloister of the contemplatives responds to the need, perceived as a priority, to remain with the Lord.

161. With the name cloister, we mean the monastic space separated from the outside and reserved for the nuns, in which the presence of strangers can only be admitted in case of necessity. It must be a space of silence and recollection where the permanent search for the face of God can develop, according to the charism of the Institute.

162. The cloister evokes that *cell of the heart* where each one is called to live in union with the Lord. Accepted as a gift and a choice as a free response to love, it is the place of spiritual communion with God and neighbor, where the limitation of space and contacts works to the advantage of the internalization of evangelical values[102].

[102] Cf. *Jn* 13:34; *Mt* 5:3.8.

163. The cloister is not only an ascetic means of immense value, but a way of living the Passover of Christ, as a joyful proclamation and prophetic anticipation of the possibility offered to each person and to the whole of humanity to live solely for God, in Christ Jesus[103].

164. In the monasteries of nuns, the cloister must be understood in a positive sense as a space for the use and intimacy of the nuns who live the contemplative life, a space of domestic and family life, within which the community lives fraternal life in its most intimate dimension.

165. In monasteries of nuns, the cloister, in a privative sense, is to be considered as a space to be protected, to prevent access by strangers.

166. The modality of separation from the outside of the space exclusively reserved for the nuns must be material and effective, not just symbolic or spiritual. It is the responsibility of the Conventual Chapter of the monastery to determine the modality of separation from the outside.

167. Each monastery is obliged to maintain its primarily or predominantly contem-

[103] Cf. *Rm* 6:11.

plative physiognomy with all solicitude, engaging in a special way to create and live an area of external and interior silence in prayer[104], in asceticism, and fervent spiritual progress, in the careful celebration of the liturgy, in fraternal life in common, in regular observance, and in the discipline of separation from the world.

II. The Means of Communication

168. The legislation concerning the means of social communication, in all the variety in which it is presented today, aims at safeguarding recollection and silence: in fact, it is possible to empty contemplative silence when the cloister is filled with noises, news, and words. Recollection and silence are of great importance for the contemplative life as "*the necessary space for listening and pondering His Word and the prerequisite for that gaze of faith that enables us to welcome God's presence in our own life and in that of the sisters [...] and in the events of today's world*"[105].

169. These means must therefore be used with sobriety and discretion, not only with regard to the contents but also to the quan-

[104] Cf. *VDq*, 33; art. 12.

[105] *VDq*, 33.

tity of information and the type of communication, "*that they may be at the service of formation for the contemplative life and necessary communication, and do not become occasions for wasting time or escaping from the demands of fraternal life in community, nor should they prove harmful for your vocation, or become an obstacle to your life wholly dedicated to contemplation*"[106].

170. The use of the means of communication for reasons of information, formation or work, can be allowed in the monastery, with prudent discernment, for common utility, according to the provisions of the Conventual Chapter contained in the community plan of life.

171. The nuns procure necessary information on the Church and the world, not with a multiplicity of news, but knowing how to grasp the essential in the light of God, to bring it to prayer in harmony with the heart of Christ.

III. The Cloister

172. Every single monastery of nuns or female monastic Congregation, according to can. 667, § 3 CJC and of the present Instruc-

[106] *VDq*, 34.

tion, conforms to papal cloister or defines it in the Constitutions or in another code of the proper law, respecting its own character[107].

173. The diocesan Bishop or the religious Ordinary oversees the observance of the cloister in the monasteries entrusted to their respective care, helping the Superior, who is responsible for its immediate custody.

174. In derogation from the provision of can. 667, § 4 CJC, the diocesan Bishop, as well as the religious Ordinary, does not intervene in granting dispensation from the cloister[108].

175. In derogation of the provisions of can. 667, § 4 CJC, the dispensation from the cloister rests solely with the Major Superior who, in the event that such dispensation exceeds fifteen days, can grant it only after having obtained the consent of her Council[109].

176. The limitation in the Instruction *Verbi Sponsa*[110] has been repealed; for just cause

[107] Cf. *VDq*, 31.

[108] Exemption approved by the Holy Father in a specific form.

[109] Exemption approved by the Holy Father in a specific form.

[110] "It should be noted that the norm of can. 665, § 1, on permanence outside the Institute, does not regard enclosed nuns", *Verbi Sponsa*, n. 17, § 2.

the Major Superior, according to the norm of can. 665, § 1 CJC, with the consent of her Council, may authorize the absence from the monastery of a nun with solemn vows for not more than a year, after hearing the diocesan Bishop or the competent religious Ordinary.

177. In derogation of can. 686, § 2 CJC, the Major Superior, with the consent of her Council, can grant the indult of exclaustration to a nun professed with solemn vows, for not more than a year, after the consent of the Ordinary of the place where the nun will have to live, and after having heard the opinion of the diocesan Bishop or of the competent religious Ordinary[111].

178. In derogation of can. 686, § 2 CJC, an extension of the indult of exclaustration can be granted by the Federal President with the consent of her Council, for a nun professed with solemn vows of a monastery of the Federation for a period of no more than two years[112].

179. For this concession, the Federal President before presenting the matter to the Fed-

[111] Exemption approved by the Holy Father in a specific form.

[112] Exemption approved by the Holy Father in a specific form.

eral Council, must obtain the written opinion of the Major Superior of the nun professing solemn vows who is asking for the extension of the indult, expressed collegially together with the Council of the monastery, with the prior consent of the Ordinary of the place where the nun will have to live, and having acquired the opinion of the diocesan Bishop or of the competent religious Ordinary.

180. Any further extension of the indult of exclaustration is reserved solely to the Holy See[113].

181. During the canonical visit, the Visitators are required to verify the observance of all the elements proper to the contemplative life as described in the Constitution *Vultum Dei quaerere*[114] with particular reference to the aspect of separation from the world.

182. The Church, because of the highest esteem it nourishes towards their vocation, encourages the nuns to live faithfully and with a sense of responsibility the spirit and the discipline of the cloister to promote in the community a fruitful and complete orientation towards the contemplation of God One and Triune.

[113] Cf. can. 686, § 1 CJC.
[114] Cf. *VDq*, 12-37.

IV. Papal Cloister

183. The papal cloister, established in 1298 by Boniface VIII, is that "*in conformity with the norms given by the Apostolic See*"[115] and excludes external works of apostolate.

184. If Pius XII had distinguished it in major and minor papal cloister, [116] the *Code of Canon Law* recognizes only one type of papal cloister, which is observed in the monasteries of nuns entirely dedicated to the contemplative life[117].

185. Papal cloister for nuns means the recognition of the specificity of an entirely contemplative life which, by individually developing the spirituality of the marriage with Christ, becomes a sign and realization of the exclusive union of the Church Bride with her Lord.

186. A real separation from the world, primarily marked by silence and solitude[118], expresses and protects the integrity and identity of wholly contemplative life, so that it may be faithful to its specific charism and to the sound traditions of the Institute.

[115] Can. 667, § 3 CJC.

[116] Cf. *SCE*, art. IV, nn. 1-2; *Inter praeclara* VI-X.

[117] Cf. *VDq*, 31.

[118] Cf. *VDq*, 33.

187. A wholly contemplative life, to be considered of papal cloister, must be fundamentally ordered to the attainment of union with God in contemplation.

188. An Institute is considered to be of wholly contemplative life if:

a) its members direct all activities, both interior and exterior, to the intense and continuous search for union with God in the monastery and to the contemplation of His face;

b) it excludes external and direct tasks of apostolate and ordinarily, physical participation in events and ministries of the ecclesial community. This participation, subject to the consent of the Conventual Chapter, must be permitted only on special occasions by the diocesan Bishop or by the religious Ordinary of the monastery;

c) it implements separation from the world, according to concrete modalities established by the Conventual Chapter, in a radical, concrete, and effective way and not simply symbolic, in accordance with the universal and proper law, in line with the Institute's charism.

V. Norms Regarding Papal Cloister

189. Given the variety of Institutes dedicated to a wholly contemplative life and of their traditions, in addition to what is established in this Instruction, some modalities of separation from the world are left to the Constitutions or other codes of the Institute's proper law which, in line with its own charism, can also establish stricter rules concerning the cloister, which must be approved by the Apostolic See.

190. The law of papal cloister extends to the dwelling and to all the interior and exterior spaces of the monastery reserved exclusively for the nuns in which the presence of strangers can be admitted only in case of necessity. It must be a space of silence and recollection, facilitated by the absence of external works, where the permanent search for the face of God can develop more easily, according to the Institute's charism.

191. The participation of the faithful in liturgical celebrations in the church or oratory of the monastery or in the *lectio divina* does not allow the exit of the nuns from papal cloister nor the entry of the faithful into the nuns' choir, except in special cases at the judgment of the conventual Chapter.

192. By virtue of papal cloister law, the nuns, novices, and postulants must live within the cloister of the monastery, and it is not lawful for them to leave, except in the cases contemplated by law nor is it permissible for anyone to enter the cloister of the monastery, except for the foreseen cases.

193. In monasteries of wholly contemplative life, the legislation on separation from the world of external sisters, if contemplated by the Constitutions or other codes of the Institute's own law, is defined by particular law.

194. The granting of permission to enter and leave the papal enclosure always requires a just cause, dictated by the true necessity of the individual nuns or of the monastery: this is required to protect the necessary conditions for a wholly contemplative life and, on the part of the nuns, of consistency with the vocational choice.

195. Where it is customary, the use of writing entries and exits in a book can be preserved, at the discretion of the Conventual Chapter, also as a contribution to the knowledge of the life and history of the monastery.

196. It is up to the Major Superior of the monastery to safeguard immediately the cloister, to guarantee the concrete conditions of separation from the world, and to promote, within the monastery, the love for silence, recollection, and prayer.

197. It is up to the Major Superior to express her judgment on the opportuneness of the entrances and exits from the papal cloister, evaluating with prudent discretion the necessity, in the light of the wholly contemplative vocation, as established by the Constitutions or other text of the proper law and prescribed by the present Instruction.

198. It is up to the Major Superior of the monastery with papal cloister to appoint a nun professed with solemn vows for the service of the porter's lodge and, if the law does not contemplate the presence of external nuns, to allow a sister to perform the services of the external sisters for a limited period of time.

199. The entire community is responsible for the moral obligation of protection, promotion, and observance of papal cloister, so that secondary or subjective motivations do not prevail over the purpose of this type of separation.

200. Leaving the papal cloister, unless with particular indults of the Holy See or in case of danger, is permitted by the Major Superior in ordinary cases, regarding the health of the nuns, the assistance of the infirm nuns, participation in courses of initial and ongoing formation meetings organized by the Federation or by another monastery, the exercise of civil rights, and those necessities of the monastery which cannot be provided for any other way.

201. To send novices or professed nuns with temporary vows when necessary to perform part of their formation in another monastery of the Institute, as well as to make temporary or definitive transfers to other monasteries of the same Institute, the Major Superior expresses her consent, with the intervention of the Council or of the Conventual Chapter according to the Constitutions or of another code of the proper law.

202. Entry into papal cloister is permitted, except for special indults of the Holy See, to Cardinals who may bring with them someone accompanying them, to Nuncios and Apostolic Delegates in places subject to their jurisdiction, to Visitators during the canonical visitation, to the diocesan Bishop[119], to the competent religious Ordinary, and to

[119] Cf. can. 667, § 4 CJC.

other persons at the judgment of the Major Superior and for a just cause.

203. Furthermore, entry into the papal cloister is allowed, subject to the permission of the Superior:

a) to the priest to administer the sacraments to the sick, to assist those who are chronically or seriously ill, to celebrate Mass for them sometimes, for liturgical processions, and funerals;

b) to those whose jobs or skills are necessary to attend to the nuns' health, for formation, and to provide for the needs of the monastery;

c) to their aspirants and passing nuns, also from other institutes of contemplative life.

VI. The Cloister Defined in the Constitutions

204. The monasteries which associate with the contemplative life some activity for the benefit of the people of God or practice wider forms of hospitality in line with the tradition of their own Institute, define their cloister in the Constitutions or in another code of the proper law.

A. *Constitutional Cloister*

205. The constitutional cloister, which has replaced in the Code of Canon Law the minor papal cloister of Pius XII, is a type of cloister regarding nuns who profess the contemplative life by associating "*some legitimate work of apostolate or Christian charity*"[120].

206. The name of constitutional cloister means the monastic space separated from the outside which, as a minimum, must include that part of the monastery of farm land or gardens reserved exclusively to the nuns, where only in case of necessity can the presence of externs be admitted. It must be a space of silence and recollection, where the permanent search for the face of God can develop, according to the charism of the Institute, in consideration of the works of apostolate or charity exercised by the nuns.

207. This type of cloister, "*appropriate to the proper character and defined by the Constitutions*"[121] is approved by the Apostolic See that approves the Constitutions or another code of the Institute's own law.

[120] Cf. *PC* 9.

[121] Cf. can. 667, § 3 CJC.

B. *Monastic Cloister*

208. To the expressions papal cloister and constitutional cloister, known from the Code of Canon Law, St. John Paul II in the post-synodal apostolic exhortation *Vita Consacrata*[122] added a third one, *monastic cloister.*

209. Before *Vita Consacrata* this expression had been used to define the cloister of the monks[123], more rigorous than that common to all religious[124], but less rigid than the papal one and comparable, in some respects, to the constitutional cloister of nuns.

210. For monasteries of contemplative nuns, the monastic cloister, while retaining the character of a more rigorous discipline than the common one, makes it possible to associate the primary function of divine worship with wider forms of reception and hospitality[125].

211. The monastic cloister, as described in the Constitutions or in another code of the proper law, is a special expression of the constitutional cloister.

[122] *VC* 59.

[123] Cf. can. 667, § 2 CJC.

[124] Cf. can. 667, § 1 CJC.

[125] Cf. *VDq*, 31.

VII. Regulations Regarding Constitutional Cloister

212. It is the responsibility of the Major Superior of the monastery, with the consent of her Council, to clearly determine the extent of the constitutional cloister, to limit it, and to modify it for just cause.

213. By virtue of the law of constitutional cloister, the nuns, novices, and postulants must live within the cloister of the monastery, and it is not permissible for them to leave, except in the cases contemplated by law, nor is it permissible for anyone to enter the cloister of the monastery outside of the foreseen cases and without the permission of the Superior.

214. The participation of the faithful in liturgical celebrations in the church or in the monastery or *lectio divina* in another suitable place of the monastery, allows the exit of the nuns from constitutional cloister remaining within the same monastery, while the entrance of the faithful is always forbidden in the part of the house subject to this type of cloister.

215. Every nun is co-responsible and must contribute, with great esteem for silence and solitude, to ensure that the external regulation of constitutional cloister preserves that fundamental inner value, through which the cloister is a source of spiritual life and witness to the presence of God.

216. They can enter the constitutional cloister of the monastery, with the consent of the Major Superior:

a) the people needed to serve the community from a spiritual, formative, and material point of view;

b) the nuns from other communities who are passing through or are guests in the monastery;

c) young women in vocational discernment.

217. The Major Superior of the monastery may permit exits from the constitutional cloister for a just cause, taking into account the indications given by the present Instruction.

218. The Major Superior of the monastery with constitutional cloister appoints nuns for the service of doorkeeper and of the guesthouse and authorizes some nuns to work in the monastery's works or workshops outside the sphere of the cloister, regulating their stay outside it.

IV.
FORMATION

219. A nun becomes with full rights a member of the community of the monastery *sui juris* and participates in its spiritual and temporal goods with the profession of solemn vows, the free and definitive response to the call of the Holy Spirit.

220. The candidates prepare themselves for solemn profession passing through the various stages of the monastic life, during which they receive an adequate formation and, although in a different degree, they are part of the community of the monastery.

I. General Principles

221. Formation in contemplative monastic life is based on a personal encounter with the Lord. It begins with the call of God and the decision of each one to follow, according to her own charism, the footsteps of Christ, as His disciple, under the action of the Holy Spirit.

222. While the acquisition of knowledge remains important, formation in the consecrated life, and particularly in contemplative monastic life, consists above all in identifying with Christ. In fact, it is a question of "*a progressive assimilation of Christ's sentiments towards the Father*"[126], to the point of being able to say with St. Paul: "*For me, to live is Christ*"[127].

223. Both the candidates and the nuns must bear in mind that in the formation process, it is not so much a matter of acquiring concepts, as "*of knowing the love of Christ that goes beyond all knowledge*"[128]. All this makes the formation process last a lifetime and every nun always feels she is in formation.

224. Formation as a continuous process of growth and conversion that involves the whole person must favor the development of the human, Christian, and monastic dimension of the candidates and nuns, radically living the Gospel, so that one's life becomes a prophecy.

225. Formation for the contemplative monastic life must be integral, that is, taking the person as a whole into account so that

[126] *VC* 65.

[127] *Fil* 1:21.

[128] *Ef* 3:19.

she develops her own psychic, moral, affective, and intellectual gifts harmoniously and becomes actively involved in community life. None of these dimensions of the person must remain excluded from the scope of either initial or ongoing formation.

226. Contemplative monastic formation must be organic, gradual, and coherent in its various stages, as it is called to promote the development of the person in a harmonious and progressive way, in full respect of the uniqueness of each one.

227. Under the action of the Holy Spirit, both candidates and nuns are the main protagonists of their formation and responsible for accepting and internalizing all the values of the monastic life.

228. For this reason, the formation process must be attentive to the uniqueness of each sister and to the mystery that she bears in herself and to her particular gifts, to foster her growth through self-knowledge and the search for the will of God.

229. In initial formation, the figure of the formator is particularly important. In fact, even if "*God the Father is the formator par excellence*", however "*in this artisan work He uses human mediations*" among which are the formators, "*whose main mission is to show the beauty of following the Lord and the value of the charism in which it is accomplished*"[129].

230. It is the responsibility of the individual monastery and of the Federation to pay particular attention to the selection of the formators and to take care of their formation[130].

II. Ongoing Formation

231. For ongoing formation, we mean an itinerary of the whole of life[131], both personal and community, "*which must lead to configuration to the Lord Jesus and the assimilation of His feelings in His total oblation to the Father*"[132]. It is therefore a process of continuous conversion of the heart, "*an intrinsic requirement of religious consecration*"[133], and the need for creative fidelity to one's own vocation. Ongoing formation is the humus of initial formation[134].

232. As such, ongoing formation must be considered as a priority both in the plan of

[129] *VC* 66.

[130] Cf. *VDq*, art. 3, § 3.

[131] Cf. can. 661 CJC.

[132] *VDq*, 13.

[133] *VC* 69.

[134] Cf. *VDq*, 3, § 1.

community life and in the plan of life of each nun.

233. The purpose of ongoing formation is to nourish and preserve fidelity, both of the individual nun and of the community, and to bring to completion what was begun in initial formation, so that the consecrated person can express fully her own gift in the Church, according to a specific charism.

234. What characterizes this stage compared to the others is the lack of ulterior short-term goals, and this can have a psychological impact: there is nothing left to prepare for, but only a daily life to be lived in the full gift of oneself to the Lord and to the Church.

235. Ongoing formation takes place in the context of daily life: in prayer and work, in the world of relationships, particularly in fraternal life in community, and in rapport with the outside, according to the contemplative vocation.

236. Ongoing formation cultivates the spiritual, doctrinal, and professional capacity, the updating and maturation of the contemplative, so that she can carry out her service to the monastery, to the Church, and to the world in an ever more appropriate manner, according to this form of life and the indications of the Apostolic Constitution *Vultum Dei quaerere.*

237. Every nun is encouraged to take responsibility for her own human, Christian, and charismatic growth, through the personal plan of life, dialog with the sisters of the monastic community, and in particular, with her Major Superior, as well as through spiritual direction and appropriate studies contemplated in the *Guidelines* for Contemplative Monastic Life.

238. Each community, together with the community plan, is called to develop a systematic and integral permanent formation program which embraces the whole existence of the person[135]. This program will be structured taking into account the different seasons of life[136] and of the various services exercised by nuns, especially by Superiors and formators[137].

239. The Major Superior promotes the ongoing formation of the community through the Conventual Chapter, the days of retreat, the annual spiritual exercises, the sharing of the Word of God, periodic revi-

[135] Cf. *VC* 60

[136] Cf. *VC* 70.

[137] Cf. *VDq*, art. 3, § 1; art. 7, § 1.

sions of life, recreations in common, study days, personal dialog with the sisters, fraternal encounters.

240. It is the responsibility of the Major Superior and of each member of the community to ensure that fraternal life is formative and helps each sister on her journey towards total configuration with Christ, the ultimate goal of the whole formation process[138], and to manifest at every moment of her life "*full and joyous belonging to Christ*"[139].

241. Notwithstanding that the ordinary place of ongoing formation is her own monastery and that fraternal life must favor the sisters' formation journey [140], in order to ensure a more adequate ongoing formation, collaboration between different monastic communities is warmly recommended, using the appropriate means of communication [141].

III. Instruments of Ongoing Formation

242. Surely the first instrument of ongoing formation for all consecrated persons, even more so for contemplatives, is care of

[138] Cf. *VC* 65.

[139] *VDq*, 13.

[140] Cf. *VDq*, 14.

[141] Cf. *VDq*, 34.

the *life of prayer*: liturgies well prepared and dignified, according to the possibility of the community; fidelity to moments of personal prayer to guarantee that space where one can establish an intimate relationship with the Lord; care of the relationship with the Word, through personal *lectio* and community *collatio*, when possible[142].

243. Care and attention to the sacrament of reconciliation and spiritual direction, attention to the choice of confessors prepared to support and accompany the journey of a community of contemplative life with discretion, wisdom, and prudence[143].

244. *Intellectual formation* must be guaranteed through a plan established by the community that possibly takes into account the cultural level of all, so that everyone can gather something useful for their own journey.

245. Also useful and important are the formation courses common to several monasteries of the same charismatic family[144], thus, federal or inter-federal courses, without forgetting that "*formation, especially ongoing*

[142] Cf. *VDq*, 24-27.

[143] *VDq*, 23.

[144] *VDq*, 14.

formation..., has its own humus *in the community and in everyday life*"[145].

246. A climate of *genuine fraternal relationships,* marked by true charity and goodness, is fundamental for allowing each member of the community to have her own space for life and expression.

247. It is the task of each of them to find the right balance in the gift of self through *work,* so that the latter may be lived as a serene and joyful service to God and to the community. However, the community is also responsible for seeing that no one is over-burdened by particularly heavy works, which absorb the energies of the mind and body to the detriment of spiritual life. Work as such can be a way to put to good use one's talents and therefore a help for the expression of the beauty of the person; it becomes dangerous when it is absolutized and captures attention to the detriment of the spirit[146].

248. *Ascetic means* must not be neglected that are of the tradition of each spirituality, as a way of curbing the instincts of one's own nature and channeling them towards

[145] *VDq,* 14.
[146] Cf. *VDq,* 32.

service to the kingdom according to their own charism.[147].

249. Even the proper *information* about what is happening in the world is an important means of reviving the awareness and responsibility of one's apostolic mission through the means of communication, using them with prudence and discretion, so that it is not detrimental to the contemplative life[148].

IV. Initial Formation

250. Initial formation is the privileged time in which the sisters who are candidates for the contemplative monastic life, with a special accompaniment of the formator and the community, are initiated in the sequela of Christ, according to a particular charism, progressively assuming and integrating their particular personal gifts with the authentic and characteristic values of their vocation.

251. Initial formation is structured in three consecutive stages: the postulancy, the novitiate, and the time of temporary or junior profession, preceded by aspirancy, in which the candidates grow and mature up to

[147] Cf. *VDq*, 35.
[148] Cf. *VDq*, 34.

the definitive assumption of the monastic life in a given Institute.

252. In initial formation, it is of great importance that between the various stages there is harmony and gradualness of content. It is equally important that between initial formation and ongoing or continuous formation there is continuity and coherence, so that there is created in the subject "*the readiness to let themselves be formed every day of their lives*"[149].

253. Keeping in mind that the person is built very slowly, and that formation must be attentive to root in the heart "*the attitudes of Christ toward the Father*"[150] and the proper human, Christian, and charismatic values, "*ample time must be reserved for initial formation*"[151], "*no less than nine years and not more than twelve*"[152].

254. Activated during this time is "*a serene discernment, free from the temptations of numbers and of efficiency*"[153]. Moreover, in each monastery special attention must be paid to spiritual

[149] *VC* 69; *Starting afresh from Christ,* 15.

[150] *VC* 65.

[151] *VC* 65.

[152] *VDq*, 15.

[153] *Starting afresh from Christ,* 18.

and vocational discernment, ensuring candidates a personalized accompaniment and promoting appropriate formation itineraries[154], paying particular attention so that formation is truly integral – human, Christian, and charismatic – and touches all the dimensions of the person.

255. The establishment of international and multicultural monastic communities manifests the universality of a charism, therefore the reception of vocations coming from other Countries must be the object of adequate discernment.

256. One of the reception criteria is given by the prospect of spreading monastic life tomorrow in particular churches where this form of following Christ is not present.

257. The recruitment of candidates from other countries solely for the sake of ensuring the survival of a monastery it to be absolutely avoided[155].

258. Every monastery *sui juris*, from the moment of its erection is the place of the novitiate and of initial, permanent or ongoing formation[156].

[154] Cf. *VDq*, 15.

[155] Cf. *VDq*, art. 3, § 6.

[156] Cf. *VDq*, art. 3, § 5.

259. In the event that, as part of the canonical visit, it results that the single monastery *sui juris* cannot guarantee a quality formation, initial formation must be taken care of in another monastery of the Federation or in the initial formation place common to various monasteries[157].

260. A monastery that is founded but not yet canonically erected and the affiliated monastery are only the place of permanent or ongoing formation.

261. The founded, but not yet canonically erected monastery, may be the place of the novitiate and place of initial formation, if the conditions set out in this Instruction concerning formation are present.

A. *Aspirancy*

262. The aspirancy, considered as a first knowledge of the monastery by the candidate and the candidate by the monastery community, involves a series of contacts and times of community experience, even prolonged. This knowledge will also be useful to fill any gaps on the path of human and religious formation at this stage.

[157] Cf. *VDq*, 3, § 7.

263. It is the responsibility of the Major Superior with her Council, taking into account each individual candidate, to establish the times and ways that the aspirant will spend in the community and outside the monastery.

264. The Lord Jesus taught that whoever undertakes an important action must first carefully consider whether there "*is enough for its completion*"[158]. For this reason, those who think of beginning the journey of contemplative life must spend a certain time in reflection regarding their real ability and to first make a personal verification of the authenticity of their call to the contemplative monastic life.

265. Having "*enough*" means possessing natural and psychological gifts, normal openness to others, psychic balance, a spirit of faith, and a firm will that make it possible to spend life in community, in continence, in obedience, in poverty, and in the cloister.

266. Without these initial qualities, one cannot conclude, either on the part of the aspirant or on the part of the welcoming community, that there is a vocation to the

[158] *Lk* 14:28.

monastic and contemplative life. Therefore, throughout initial formation, but particularly during the aspirancy, particular attention must be paid to the human dimension.

267. During this time, the aspirant is entrusted by the Major Superior to a solemnly professed sister so that she may be accompanied and guided in her vocational choice.

268. The aspirancy, of a minimum duration of twelve months, may be extended according to need at the discretion of the Major Superior, after consulting her Council, but for no longer than two years.

B. *Postulancy*

269. The postulancy is a necessary stage for proper preparation for the novitiate[159], during which the candidate confirms her determination to be converted through a progressive passage from secular life to contemplative monastic life.

270. During this time, the postulant must be gradually introduced to the process of assimilation of the fundamental elements of contemplative monastic life.

[159] Cf. can. 597, § 2 CJC.

271. The postulancy offers a more direct and concrete experience of community life according to a specific charism.

272. Before admitting an aspirant to the postulancy, one must examine her state of health, if her maturity is appropriate for her age, if she has a suitable disposition, if she is sociable, solid in Christian doctrine and practice, if she aspires to the monastic life with a sincere intention, seeking the face of God at all times.

273. The postulant must be entrusted to the novice formator or to a solemnly professed nun who helps her to look within herself, who can discern if there is a real call to contemplative monastic life, and to whom the postulant can open herself with full trust.

274. The postulant, helped by the formator, is especially dedicated to her human and spiritual formation and deepens her baptismal commitment.

275. The postulancy has a minimum duration of twelve months which can be prolonged according to need by the Major Superior, having heard her Council, but it must not exceed two years.

276. During this period, the postulants live in the monastery and follow the life of the community according to the instructions of the formator and, besides being helped to know their capacity for monastic life, they can deepen themes of study or learn a trade, according to the needs of the community, as established by the Major Superior with her Council.

C. *Novitiate*

277. The novitiate is the time when the novice begins life in a given institute; her vocational discernment continues and the deepening of her own decision to follow Jesus Christ in the Church and in today's world, according to a determined charism.

278. The novitiate is the time of trial, and its objective is to lead the candidate to become more fully aware of the vocation according to a specific charism, verifying the real and concrete ability to live it with joy and generosity, particularly in reference to fraternal life in community.

279. The novitiate in monasteries of nuns has a duration of two years, the second being the canonical one, following the provisions of can. 648 CJC concerning absences.

280. During the novitiate, the novice must first of all deepen her friendship with Christ because without this she will never be able to assume and keep the promises of donation to Him and desire to grow in the knowledge of the charism that she is called to live, questioning herself if she wants to share her existence in a fraternal life in common with the sisters who make up the community of the monastery.

281. The novice obtains this through the practice of prolonged *lectio divina*, under the guidance of an expert sister who knows how to open her mind to the intelligence of the Scriptures, guided by the writings of the Fathers of the Church, and the writings and examples of life of their founders. Intimate contact with Christ must necessarily lead to a strong sacramental life and to personal prayer, to which the novice must be guided and for which adequate time must be granted.

282. Personal prayer finds its outlet in community liturgical prayer, to which the novice must devote all her best energies. In this atmosphere of love for Christ and prayer, the novice opens herself to the sisters, loves them cordially, and lives with them in fraternity.

283. The novice is guided by the formator to cultivate an authentic devotion to the Virgin Mother of God, model and patron of every consecrated life[160], and to take her as the example of a consecrated woman.

284. The spiritual edifice cannot be built without human foundations, so the novices must perfect the gifts of nature and education, and develop their own personality, feeling truly responsible for their own human, Christian, and charismatic growth.

D. *Juniorate*

285. In this stage, insertion into the life of the community is full, so the goal is to experience the capacity of the temporary professed to find a proper balance between the various dimensions of contemplative monastic life (prayer, work, fraternal relationships, study...), succeeding in creating their own personal synthesis of the charism and incarnating it in the various situations of daily life.

286. Without prejudice to what is established by the universal law concerning the valid and licit profession of temporary vows, the juniorate includes the period of initial formation from the first profession of tempo-

[160] Cf. can. 663, § 4 CJC.

rary vows to solemn profession, in which the professed continues her spiritual, doctrinal, and practical formation, according to the charism and the law proper to the Institute.

287. Temporary profession is emitted for three years and renewed annually up to the completion of five years, until a minimum of nine years of initial formation is completed.

288. If it seems opportune, the time of temporary profession can be prolonged by the Major Superior, according to the proper law and the norm of can. 657, § 2 CJC, but making sure that twelve years of initial formation are not exceeded.

289. In each monastic community, the path of initial and ongoing or continuous formation, as well as the formation of the Superior of the monasteries [161], of the formators,[162] and of the financial administrators, will be modulated according to the charism and law of the Institute, keeping in mind the *Guidelines* published by the Congregation for Institutes of Consecrated Life and Societies of Apostolic Life, as a continuation and completion of the present Instruction.

[161] Cf. *VDq*, art. 7, § 1.

[162] Cf. *VDq*, art. 3, §§ 3 and 4.

FINAL DISPOSITIONS

• The present Instruction does not only concern future things[163] but it applies in the present to all monasteries of Latin rite nuns from the moment of its publication.

• The provisions of the Apostolic Constitution *Vultum Dei quaerere* for all the monasteries concerning the obligation to enter a Federation of monasteries also applies to other structures of communion such as the Association of monasteries or the Conference of monasteries.

• This obligation also applies to monasteries associated with a male institute or united in an autonomous monastic congregation.

• Individual monasteries must comply with this within one year of the publication of this Instruction, unless they have been legitimately dispensed.

• Once the time has passed, this Dicastery will assign monasteries to Federations or to other existing structures of communion.

[163] Cf. can. 9 CJC.

• The decisions that, after appropriate consultation and prior discussion in the Congress of the Dicastery, will be taken by this Congregation for Institutes of Consecrated Life and Societies of Apostolic Life towards a monastery of nuns relating to the call for an apostolic visit, to the commissioning, to the suspension of autonomy and to the suppression of a monastery will be presented on a monthly basis to the Roman Pontiff for approval in a specific form.

CONCLUSION

With this Instruction, this Dicastery intends to confirm the high appreciation of the Church for the contemplative monastic life and its solicitude to safeguard the authenticity of this unique form of the *sequela Christi*.

On March 16, 2018, the Holy Father approved the present document of the Congregation for Institutes of Consecrated Life and Societies of Apostolic Life and authorized its publication.

On the same date, the Holy Father approved the present Instruction in specific form:

- nos. 52, 81 *d*) and 108, in derogation from can. 638, § 4 CJC;
- no. 83 *g*) in derogation from can 667, § 4 CJC;
- no. 111 in derogation from can. 628, § 2, 1º CJC;
- no. 130 in derogation from can. 686, § 2 CJC;
- nos. 174 e 175 in derogation from can. 667, § 4 CJC;

• no. 176, which abrogates the restriction of *Verbi Sponsa* n. 17, § 2;

• nos. 177 e 178 in derogation from can. 686, § 2 CJC;

• final Dispositions.

From the Vatican, April 1, 2018
Solemnity of the Resurrection of the Lord

João Braz Card. de Aviz
Prefect

✠ José Rodríguez Carballo, O.F.M.
Archbishop Secretary

INDEX

www.ingramcontent.com/pod-product-compliance
Lightning Source LLC
LaVergne TN
LVHW040347160726
843469LV00039B/629
9788826606491